Do Flying Fish Really Fly?

ANSWERING KIDS' QUESTIONS

by Ellen Labrecque

PEBBLE

a capstone imprint

Pebble Emerge is published by Pebble, an imprint of Capstone.
1710 Roe Crest Drive
North Mankato, Minnesota 56003
www.capstonepub.com

Library of Congress Cataloging-in-Publication Data
Names: Labrecque, Ellen, author.
Title: Do flying fish really fly? : answering kids' questions / by Ellen Labrecque.

Description: North Mankato, MN : Capstone Press, [2021] | Series: Questions and answers about animals | Includes bibliographical references and index. | Audience: Ages 6-8 | Audience: Grades 2-3 | Summary: "Everyone knows that fish swim. But are there fish that fly? You have questions and this book has the answers. Find out about the lives of certain fish and their unique abilities to move through the water"-- Provided by publisher.
Identifiers: LCCN 2020036388 (print) | LCCN 2020036389 (ebook) | ISBN 9781977131645 (hardcover) | ISBN 9781977132710 (paperback) | ISBN 9781977154118 (pdf) | ISBN 9781977155825 (kindle edition)
Subjects: LCSH: Flyingfishes--Juvenile literature.
Classification: LCC QL638.E9 L33 2021 (print) | LCC QL638.E9 (ebook) | DDC 597/.66--dc23
LC record available at https://lccn.loc.gov/2020036388
LC ebook record available at https://lccn.loc.gov/2020036389

Image Credits
Alamy: BIOSPHOTO, 19, blickwinkel, 7, Paulo Oliveira, 11; Capstone Studio: Karon Dubke, 21; Getty Images: Sylvain Cordier, 15; imagequestmarine.com: Peter Parks, 17; Minden Pictures: Alex Mustard, 8; Shutterstock: Agami Photo Agency, 9, COZ, Cover, Graham D Elliott, 5, owatta, design element, Rvector, design element, Sameer Nemane, 13

Editorial Credits
Editor: Megan Peterson; Designer: Ted Williams; Media Researcher: Jo Miller; Production Specialist: Spencer Rosio

Printed and bound in the USA.   3837

Table of Contents

Words in **bold** are in the glossary.

Can Fish Fly?

You and your family are sailing in a boat on the ocean. The salty air is warm. The wind blows your hair. You feel the hot sun on your skin.

Look out! A fish soars through the air. It hits your arm! Fish fly all around you. Some zoom by your head. Are you dreaming? Or can fish really fly?

A Bird? A Plane? A Fish?

There are more than 30,000 kinds of fish. Fish are **vertebrates**. They have backbones. They live in water and breathe through **gills**. Fish swim with **fins**.

Some fish can get into the air! There are more than 40 kinds of flying fish. Flying fish **glide** through the air. They don't flap their fins like wings. They stretch them out and soar.

Take Off

Flying fish fly to get away from dolphins, tuna, and other **predators**. To take off, flying fish swim quickly. They swish their tails more than 50 times per second!

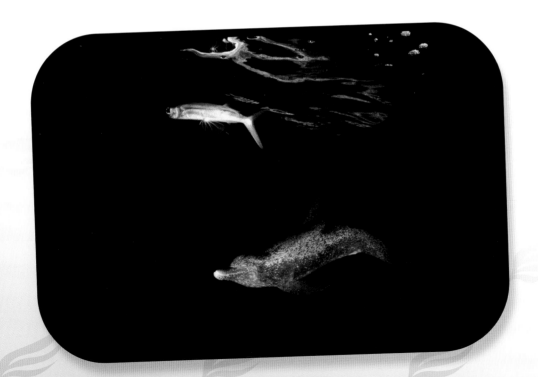

Flying fish have forked tails. Their tails help them break through the water's surface. They push the fish up into the air. Then the fish spread their large fins to glide.

Up in the Air

Flying fish are fast flyers. They can reach speeds of 35 miles (56 kilometers) per hour. They can glide more than 650 feet (200 meters).

Flying fish can stay in the air up to 15 seconds. But they must be careful. They might become lunch for seabirds! Flying fish are not safe anywhere.

11

Landing

As flying fish lose speed, they fall back to the water. Sometimes they dive underwater to hide from birds.

Other times, flying fish skim the water with their tails. Their tails move back and forth quickly. They give the fish power to lift off again.

Warm Water Only

Flying fish live in oceans. They like warm air and warm water. They can't fly when they get too cold. Their muscles don't work as well.

The island of Barbados is in the Caribbean Sea. It is called "The Land of the Flying Fish." Big groups of flying fish swim in its waters.

Flying Fish Babies

Flying fish lay their eggs on sea plants. The eggs stick to the plants. Some baby flying fish **hatch** in a few days. Others take two weeks.

Baby flying fish have whiskers to **blend** in with the plants. They can fly soon after birth.

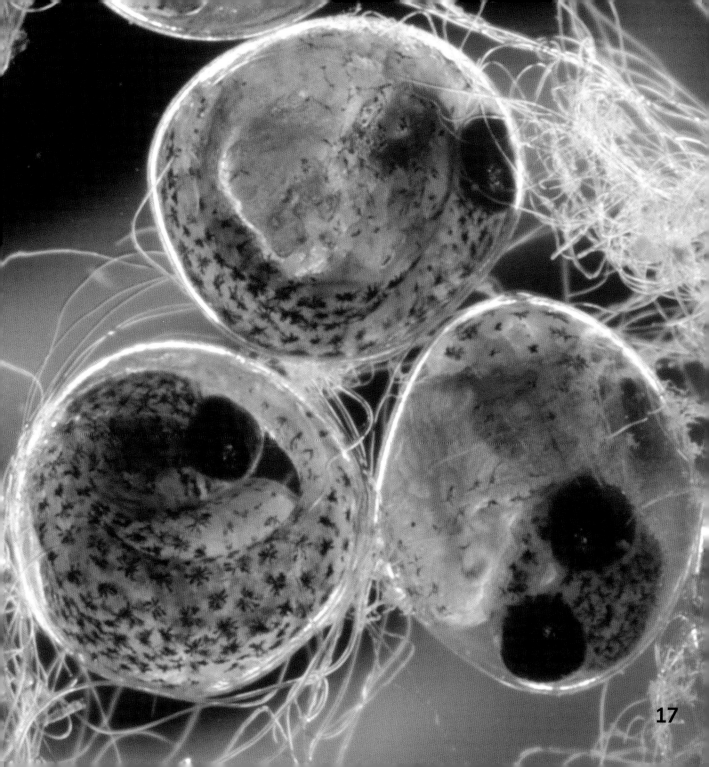

17

The Wonder of Flying Fish

Flying fish have been around for millions of years. But they didn't always fly. These fish slowly learned to fly over time.

Their fins grew larger to help them glide. Flying helped the fish stay safe. And they have been flying ever since!

19

Make Your Own Flying Fish

What You Need:

- ruler
- scissors
- construction paper

What You Do:

1. Cut a strip of construction paper about 1 inch (2.5 cm) wide. It should be about 12 inches (30 cm) long.

2. Cut a small slit near both ends of the strip. Do not cut all the way through. Make one cut on the left side. The other cut should be on the right side.

3. Move the ends of the strip toward each other. Slide the two slits together to make your flying fish.

4. Flip the fish up into the air. Watch it flutter down to the ground.

5. Make more fish in different colors. You can have a whole school of flying fish!

Glossary

blend (BLEND)—to fit in with the surroundings

fin (FIN)—a body part that fish use to swim and steer in water

gill (GIL)—a body part on the side of a fish; fish use their gills to breathe

glide (GLIDE)—to move smoothly and easily

hatch (HACH)—to break out of an egg

predator (PRED-uh-tur)—an animal that hunts other animals for food

vertebrate (VUR-tuh-bruht)—an animal with a backbone

Read More

Duhaime, Darla. *Flying Fish*. Vero Beach, FL: Rourke Educational Media, 2017.

Harvey, Derek. *Did You Know?: Animals*. New York: DK/Penguin Random House, 2016.

Jenkins, Steve. *Speediest!: 19 Very Fast Animals*. Boston: Houghton Mifflin Harcourt, 2018.

Internet Sites

Kiddle: Flying Fish Facts for Kids
kids.kiddle.co/Flying_fish

National Geographic: Flying Fish
nationalgeographic.com/animals/fish/group/flying-fish/

The National Wildlife Federation: Flying Fish
nwf.org/Educational-Resources/Wildlife-Guide/Fish/Flying-Fish

Index